Spiritual Lessons Learned from My Plants

by

Geneitha Allen

Watersprings Publishing

Spiritual Lessons Learned from My Plants
Published by Watersprings Publishing,
a division of Watersprings Media House, LLC.
P.O. Box 1284, Olive Branch, MS 38654
www.waterspringsmedia.com
Contact publisher for bulk orders and permission requests.

Copyright © 2021 GENEITHA ALLEN. All rights reserved.

No part of this publication may be reproduced, distributed, or transmitted in any form or by any means, including photocopying, recording, or other electronic or mechanical methods, without the prior written permission of the publisher, except in the case of brief quotations embodied in critical reviews and certain other noncommercial uses permitted by copyright law.

Scripture quotations credited to NASB are from the New American Standard Bible, copyright © 1960, 1962, 1963, 1968, 1971, 1972, 1973, 1975, by the Lockman Foundation. Used by permission.

Scripture quotations credited to NIV are from the Holy Bible, New International Version. Copyright © 1973, 1978, 1984, 2011 by Biblica, Inc. Used by permission. All rights reserved worldwide.

Scripture quotations marked "NKJV" are taken from the New King James Version. Copyright © 1982 by Thomas Nelson, Inc. Used by permission. All rights reserved.

ISBN-13: 978-1-948877-84-8

TABLE OF CONTENTS

LESSON 1	Lessons From an Evergreen	11
LESSON 2	It Takes No Effort to Grow Weeds	15
LESSON 3	Be Careful What You Plant	19
LESSON 4	Behold, I Do a New Thing	23
LESSON 5	If It Is Not Nurtured – It Will Die!	27
LESSON 6	Everything Has Its Season	31
LESSON 7	The Euonymus – Take A Chance	35
LESSON 8	Seeing the Big Picture	39
LESSON 9	Insignificant Can Turn Into Something Beautiful	43
LESSON 10	You Don't Have the Final Word	47
LESSON 11	You Must Be Watered On a Daily Basis	51
LESSON 12	Are Not Two Sparrows Sold For a Penny?	55
LESSON 13	It's All About Perspective	59
LESSON 14	He Knows How Much You Can Bear	63
About The Author		67

> "The heavens declare the glory of God;
> the skies proclaim the work of his hands.
> Day after day they pour forth speech;
> night after night they reveal knowledge.
> They have no speech, they use no words;
> no sound is heard from them.
> Yet their voice goes out into all the earth,
> their words to the ends of the world."
>
> **PSALM 19:1-4, NIV**

Introduction

Learning is a lifelong experience. For many years I have kept a prayer journal. Every morning as I write my prayers, I ask God for wisdom and for Him to speak to me in clear tones that I will be able to not only hear Him, but to understand what He is saying to me, and to know with certainty that He is the one speaking. At the end of each day, we may go through our experiences and try to decipher what God said to us during that day, and if we obeyed His instructions, or followed in the path He was leading. Sometimes we miss what God is trying to tell us, not because He hasn't spoken, but because we are looking for the booming voice that will speak to us like in the movies. God does not always speak to us that way. He can if He so chooses because He is God. However, most of the time God speaks to us using the everyday, mundane things of life, in the same way He used parables in the past; parables that used common and everyday things that the people of those times were familiar with and could relate to. God is still speaking to us using the everyday things of life that impact us individually. Because different things are important to each of us, He will speak to us using the things that we are each familiar with. As an individual who is enamored with nature, plants, and gardening, God speaks to me using those things. *Spiritual Lessons Learned From My Plants* are just that, God speaking to me using the everyday and ordinary things in my life that I can understand. The lessons that come through in the various scenarios allowed me to take a look at my life in the context of where God fits in it and what is needed by His grace, to maintain that relationship with Him. As you read them, my prayer is that they will allow you to reflect on your own experiences and what God is doing in your life, and that you will open up your heart's ears and allow God to speak to you in the language that you understand.

"Speak, LORD, for your servant is listening."
1 SAMUEL 3:9, NIV

*Spiritual Lessons
Learned from My Plants*

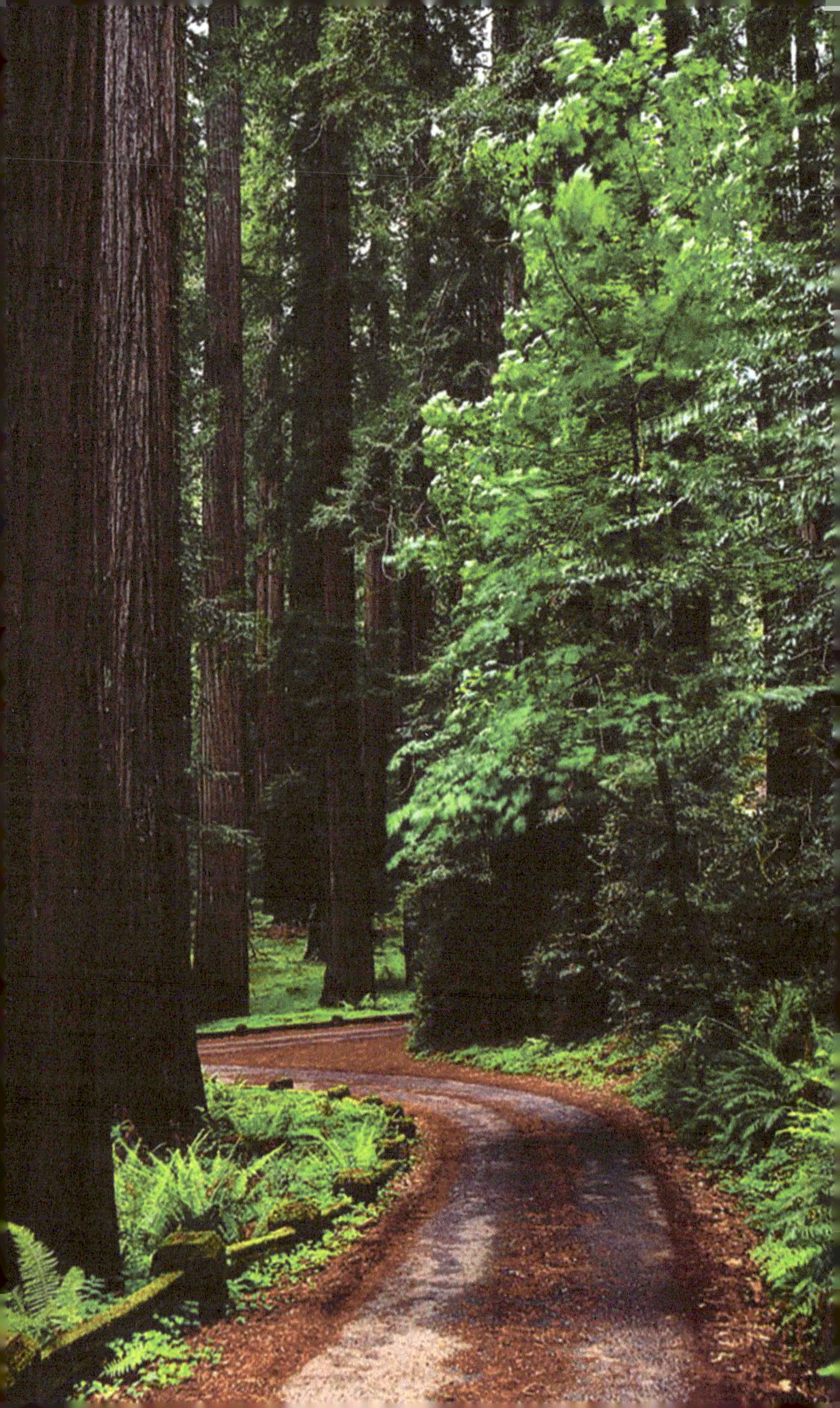

LESSON 1

Lessons From an Evergreen

> **Create in me a clean heart, O God and renew a steadfast spirit within me.**
> PSALM 51:10, NKJV

I am not an expert gardener by any means, but I love gardening. I am what you might call a "putterer". When we bought our home over three decades ago, I started puttering. I planted roses, flowering shrubs, and many evergreens, most of them cedars. I chose cedars because they are hardy, and it would take a lot for me to kill them.

When you are a putterer, you need that assurance! I remember digging the holes with the kitchen knife and planting the tiny seedlings.

It is hard to believe they were all that small because they are now over 10 feet tall. Late one summer, I decided to do some pruning and learned a valuable lesson. The trees looked beautiful and green on the outside; just as they have always looked over the years. However, when I started pruning, I was amazed at what I saw on the inside; the trees were slowly dying. They looked green on the outside but were bone dry on the inside.

By the end of the pruning, there were bags of dried leaves and branches, which took a considerable amount of time to remove. I was amazed they survived at all with the damage on the inside. As I removed the dead leaves, I realized that the trees were not getting enough deep watering. As a result, their roots did not run deep in the soil but ran along the surface like tentacles, searching for water.

I did some heavy pruning, and at times I felt I was hurting the trees, but it reminded me of my Christian experience.

As Christians, we sometimes look outstanding on the outside, but our insides, like the evergreen, are dry and brittle, desperately crying out for living water. So sometimes God, too, has to do some heavy "pruning" in our lives to make us the flourishing Christians we ought to be. It might be painful, but in the end, it makes us better Christians.

Unlike the evergreen, we have a choice. We are the only ones who know the state of our spiritual connection when we stand before God. Like David, we need to ask God to 'create in us a clean heart and renew a steadfast spirit within us.' (Psalm 51:10) Then we shall be like beautiful evergreens planted by the rivers.

To be what God wants us to be, it must start from the inside and flow to the outside. When our inside is clear, and all the unwanted dead leaves are gone, we can stand tall and green. Then and only then will we be ready to share the beauty for all to see. So let's make it our desire this year to be beautiful inside and out.

> "...The LORD does not look at the things people look at. People look at the outward appearance, but the LORD looks at the heart."
> **1 SAMUEL 16:7, NIV**

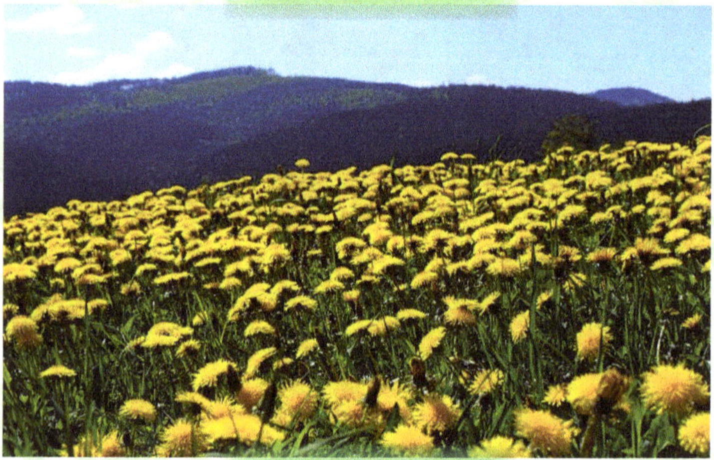

LESSON 2

It Takes No Effort to Grow Weeds

> **The righteous will never be uprooted...**
> PROVERBS 10:30, NIV

Every summer, my husband and I decide what kind of flowers we will plant in our garden for the season. As much as we love to see beautiful colors in the garden, we do not know the names of many of them. Usually, we choose based on how they look, their outward appearance, and normally based on flowers we see in greenhouses or other people's flower gardens.

Once we decide what we will plant, it takes a lot of effort to take care of them. We fertilize, weed, till the soil around the plants, and water, water, water. We came close to losing some when it got too hot in the daytime while we are at work. We came home to find them wilted and near death because of the heat.

"It" started as a little green thing with three leaves, like a clover. I didn't plant it, so I figured it must be a weed. A weed is simply a flower growing in a place that you don't want it to grow, so I uprooted it. Then I noticed that several of the same plants were popping up at different places throughout my garden. As fast as I pulled the weeds, the more they appeared. I didn't have to water them or till the soil around them, yet they still flourished. They seem to grow twice as big as the plants I had planted and labored hard to maintain. Then one day, I noticed it bloomed a little white flower; there were many of them by then. I thought to myself: this is really neat. It blooms, doesn't need a lot of work on my part, and it looks good. So, I decided not to uproot them. Big mistake!

Before I knew it, the weed was growing like crazy. It tripled in size. The little white flowers dried, dropping seeds all over the place, which grew into more of the same. These weeds now became a force to be reckoned with. They started crowding out the actual plants.

I decided it was time to get rid of them, but I had my job cut out for me. I found the effort to remove them was twice as difficult as if I had removed them when they were smaller. This weed had the strongest root system I had ever seen. It didn't grow and run along the soil's surface but sent big strong roots deep in the ground. It didn't matter if it was watered; it was there for the long haul. To get rid of it, I had to grasp it with both hands and pull with all my might. This sometimes sent me reeling back on my behind.

Now that I know what they are capable of, I pull them out before they have a chance to establish roots. This, too, reminds me of our Christian life. At times we allow little things to creep in. At first, they seem harmless and inconsequential, so we get careless and allow them to grow. At times they may seem cute and may even appear to be helpful to us at the moment. But, if left unchecked, they put down roots. Strong roots. They take over and crowd out the good things in our lives. Now, we have to grasp them with both hands to pull them out. Otherwise, they will choke out the good character traits and spoil our ministry.

Christ has given us clear instructions; we need to make conscious choices of what we plant in our lives daily. Do not allow weeds to grow, no matter how harmless they appear or how cute they seem. Do not wait for them to put down roots before you decide to pull them. Don't let them choke out the real you and prevent you from being the person God has ordained you to be.

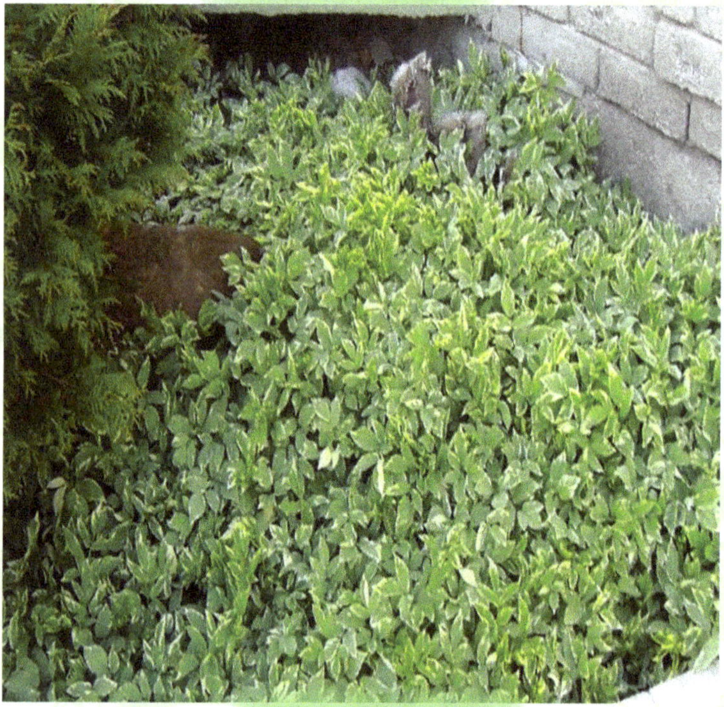

LESSON 3

Be Careful What You Plant

> **❝ Do not be deceived, God is not mocked; for whatever a man sows, that he will also reap. ❞**
> **GALATIANS 6:7, NKJV**

I first saw them in my brother's front garden. I later found out they are called Queen Ann's lace. They didn't have flowers, but I liked the color of the foliage. I liked how they covered the ground around the walkway, and I thought, These would look great on one particular area of my front lawn. I am not sure how or where I got the piece I planted, but I planted it, and it took off like wildfire.

The first year I thought it was great. It provided the cover I wanted in the area and didn't take much effort on my part.

The following year I found that the Queen was extending her borders. She was going far beyond the area I wanted her to cover. I couldn't control it. It didn't send roots deep in the ground as in the previous lesson; these roots grow just below the soil's surface and send

19

out tentacles several feet along the ground.

I have spent every summer since then trying to rid my garden of Queen Ann's Lace, but like a bad penny, she keeps coming back year after year. I have chosen one side of the garden where they will look the best and fight daily to keep them contained in that area. I am resigned to the fact that I will spend many hours each summer keeping Queen Ann's Lace to her side of the garden.

Interestingly, my brother visited me one summer, and I remarked how this plant just takes over my garden. It was only then that he told me, "Oh yeah, it is like a parasite. It takes over everything." Gee, thanks for telling me that!

Isn't that so much like sin? It is still a fact that the grass always looks greener on the other side of the fence. We sometimes covet what we see in others, and we have no idea of the devastation it will cause in our lives until we bring it in. We don't always get the truth of what it can do to us until we have embraced it. We think it is something we can contain because it seems to be working for so and so. We then embrace it, only to discover that it is not exactly what we thought it would be. It is not what we wanted, and we spend the rest of our lives trying to keep it in its place.

Make sure anything you bring into your life is what you want before embracing it. Sometimes it is difficult to decide what we should and shouldn't embrace, but God, in His infinite wisdom, gives us a full-proof way to decide.

> "...whatever is true, whatever is honorable, whatever is right, whatever is pure, whatever is lovely, whatever is commendable, if there is any excellence and if anything is worthy of praise, think about these things."
> **PHILIPPIANS 4:8, NASB**

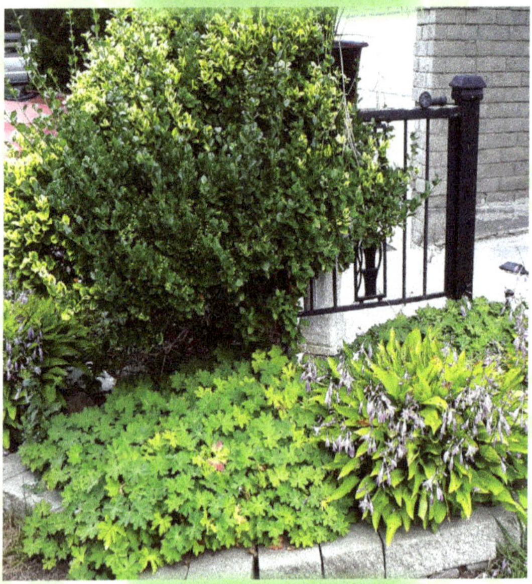

LESSON 4

Behold, I Do a New Thing

> **❝Forget the former things; do not dwell on the past. See, I am doing a new thing...❞**
> **Isaiah 43:18-19, NIV**

Winter brings with it a significant amount of snow where we live. That is the nature of winter in a snow belt! This particular winter was pretty bad. There were times when the snowbanks were so high that backing out of the driveway was like coming out of a tunnel. Fortified on both sides by thousands of white-clad soldiers.

There were times when you could see no end to the cold white stuff. But, as nature took its course, the weather eventually warmed up, and eventually, the fortified walls began to melt, albeit slowly. Before long, the beautiful blanket of white was gone, and a remarkable reality emerged.

The disappearance of the beautiful white blanket of snow, revealed in its place, a very dirty lawn, filled with rotted leaves, small branches, newspaper, and a number of other discarded items. I asked myself, where did all this garbage come from? I didn't recall them being there in the fall before the snow fell.

I couldn't bear the thought of it staying like that, so off I went to rake up the leaves and remove the trash. It was then that I noticed the tulip bulbs popping up their tiny heads, despite the filth around them. I again thought of my Christian experience. It too, was like my garden, filled with debris and unpleasant things but covered with a beautiful blanket that looks good from all outward appearance. Despite the unpleasantness in my life, and like the tulips waiting to burst into bloom; God is waiting to do a new thing with my sinful life. If I give Him a chance, He will not only bring beautiful colored tulips and hyacinths but a luscious and verdant landscape that will be beautiful to behold.

"Do not conform to the pattern of this world, but be transformed by the renewing of your mind. Then you will be able to test and approve what God's will is—His good, pleasing and perfect will."

ROMANS 12:2, NIV

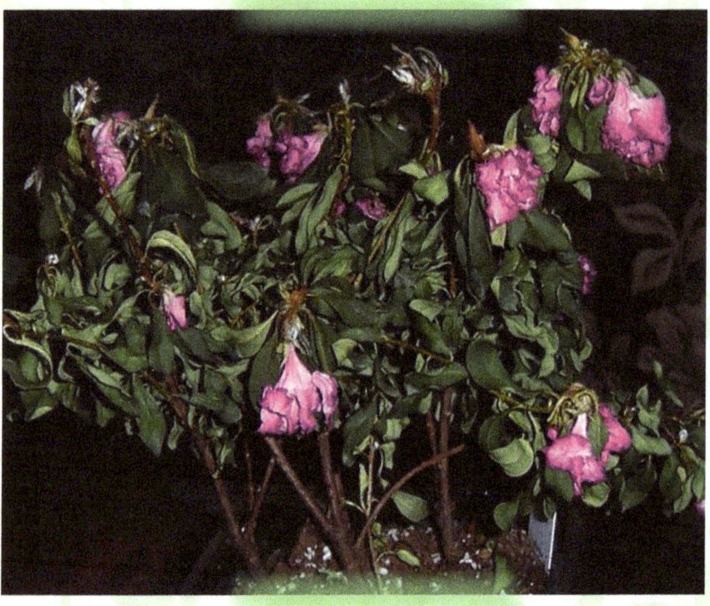

LESSON 5
If It Is Not Nurtured – It Will Die!

> **Abide in Me, and I in you. As the branch cannot bear fruit of itself unless it abides in the vine, so neither can you unless you abide in Me.**
> JOHN 15:4, NKJV

I am attracted to plants like moths to a flame. So, I walked into the "Kitchen Table," intending to buy lunch but headed straight for the beautiful azalea plant. I knew it would not survive in my office because I have no windows and the lighting is on an automatic timer.

Despite knowing this, I have purchased several plants, hoping that they would defy the laws of nature and survive by some miracle. That has not yet happened, but my hope still remains alive!

Despite knowing that, however, I had to have this plant. I bought it and enjoyed having it on my desk for a couple of days. It was now Thursday, and I knew it would not survive over the long weekend, locked away in a dark and dry office, so I took it home.

I found a perfect spot on the ledge of the bay window in my living room, which faces south. It looked beautiful.

I forgot, however, that potted plants which are normally planted in very porous soil have to be watered on a daily basis.

Well, I forgot to water it every day, and the fact that it was exposed to bright sunlight meant that whatever moisture was present dried out very quickly. By the time I realized what was happening, my beautiful Azalea had dried up. Needless to say, I was agitated.

Of course, I tried watering it, even though I realized that it would probably not make any difference. I watered it for several days, but alas, it was too late. The damage was already done, and it was irreparable. My beautiful Azalea was dead, and no amount of watering was going to bring it back to life.

This is so much like our Christian experience. Knowing Christ is a beautiful thing. When you first come to the Lord, you are on top of the world. Life seems good, and you are living the experience.

In order to remain connected to the savior, to bloom and reflect His glory, you must feed on the word of God. You cannot feed once a week, but you must immerse yourself in His word daily. You must ensure that the soil is good so that when the nutrients of the word, mixed together by the Holy Spirit, are administered to your thirsty soul daily, it will do the work making sure your life reflects the beauty of Christ's holiness. Otherwise, like the Azalea, you will shrivel up and die.

❝ Then Jesus declared, "I am the bread of life. Whoever comes to me will never go hungry, and whoever believes in Me will never be thirsty.❞

JOHN 6:35, NIV

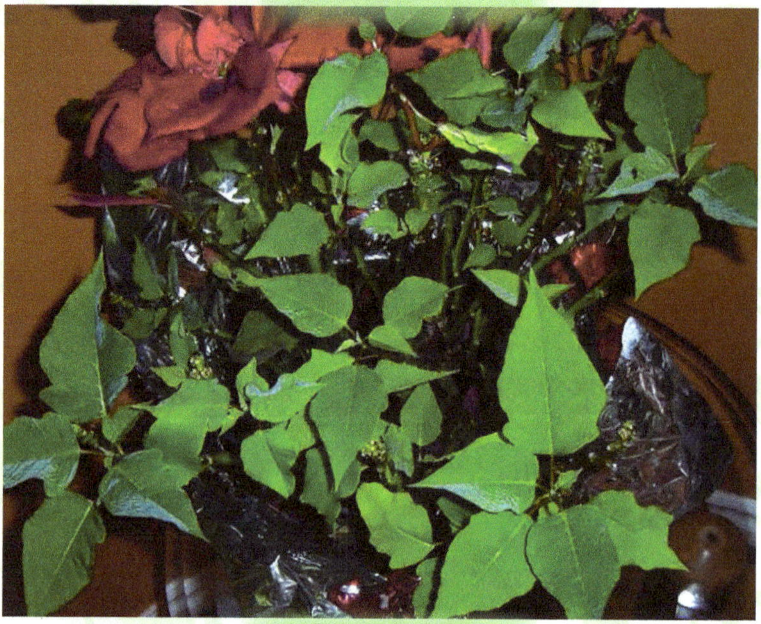

LESSON 6

Everything Has Its Season

> **There is a time for everything, and a season for every activity under the heavens.**
> ECCLESIASTES 3:1, NIV

I was given a beautiful Poinsettia at Christmas time. I took it home and set it in a prominent place in my foyer, where it could be admired as soon as you opened the front door. I admired it every day, and unlike the Azalea, I did not forget to water it. Each time I passed, I remarked on how beautiful it looked. I knew it was a seasonal plant. I have had many poinsettias, and I have tried on several occasions to make them last beyond the Christmas season. This one was so huge and beautiful; I was sure it would defy all my previous attempts and remain as a permanent plant.

As the days went by, each time I passed the plant, I would notice some dried leaves on the table. I would stick my finger in the soil to test if it was dry. As the days went by, more and more leaves started falling. Now my beautiful plant was not as lush and as thick as it used to be. I would prune it to remove the dead leaves hoping that it would encourage its survival.

My poinsettia still sits on the table in my foyer. It is still visible as you enter the door or come down the stairs. However, it is not as beautiful as it once was. Most of the foliage is gone, and the majority of the blooms are no longer there. I am still watering it, and I pick off the dead leaves each time I pass it. However, I am resigned to the fact that Christmas is over, and the plant may have already served its purpose. I finally decided to put the plant in the backyard. It now sits in a corner on the back porch, not as glorious as it used to be.

Sometimes people come into our lives for a season. When they are there, they are beautiful, the fellowship is enjoyable, and they bring sunshine to our lives. As the years progress, however, the brilliance may start to fade, and you will do all you can to infuse life into that relationship, but to no avail.

If and when this happens, don't stress. Remember that the season for that friendship or that relationship is probably just drawing to a close. So let it go with grace, and know that God will bring another beautiful one into your life for another season.

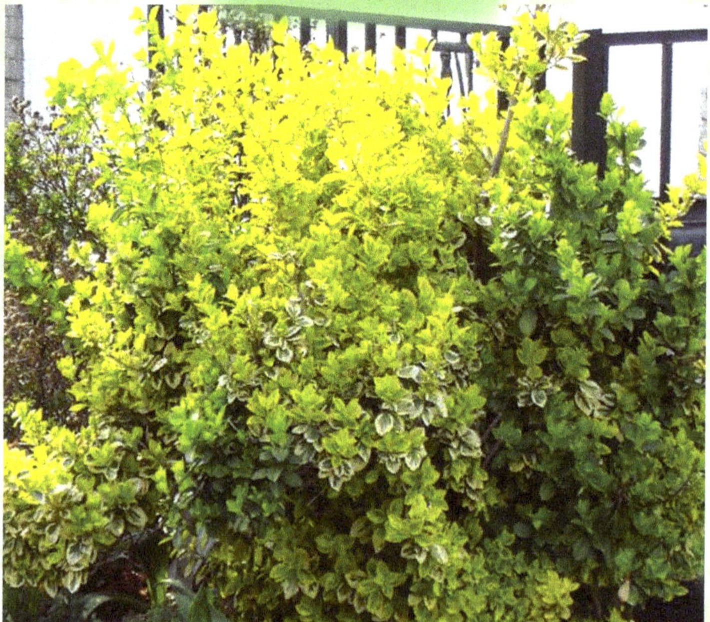

LESSON 7

The Euonymus – Take a Chance

> **For I know the plans I have for you, declares the Lord, plans to prosper you and not to harm you, plans to give you hope and a future.**
> JEREMIAH 29:11, NIV

I was so excited to move into my new house. What should I do first? I know, I will plant some trees. One of the trees I planted was a climbing Euonymus. I planted it right in the middle of the bay window. It looked great there. It never occurred to me that it would grow into a big plant and could be a problem.

After a number of years, the Euonymus did what it was intended by God to do. It grew and flourished. It was now evident that under the bay window was not the best place to have planted it. It was too close to the window, and I was concerned that the roots would be too close to the house's foundation. As the years went by, we had to change the window, which meant that the Euonymus had to go.

At first, I thought of just destroying it. Just chop it

down and throw it in the trash, but I couldn't bring myself to do it. I carefully dug up the plant and transplanted it to the bottom of the garden patch.

After I moved the plant, I remember my neighbor came over to help with the installation of the new window and commented on the plant. He said, "This plant will be dead in no time. You are wasting your time replanting it." I considered his comments but decided to leave the plant in its new position. After all, what did I have to lose?

I remember praying for the plant. "Lord, this is as important to you as it is to me, so I am committing it into your hands."

Today the euonymus is the focal point of my walkway. Resplendent, in its seasonal change between yellow and green, it is a beacon that attracts eyes and feet to my front door. Sometimes, you have to not listen to others. Instead, go with your heart, give it your best and let God do the rest. He can turn something that looks dead into a flourishing plant because only He knows the plans he has for you. Don't let others sabotage your purpose.

" But you are a chosen people, a royal priesthood, a holy nation, God's special possession, that you may declare the praises of Him who called you out of darkness into His wonderful light."

1 PETER 2:9, NIV

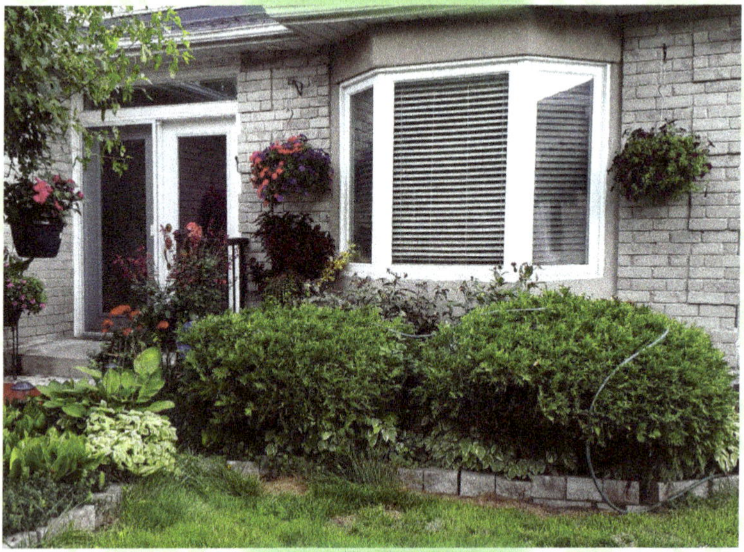

LESSON 8
Seeing the Big Picture

> ❝All who are prudent acts with knowledge…❞
> **PROVERBS 13:16, NIV**

Part of the joy of owning a new home is having a patch of ground to call my own. I can plant my garden, something I have always wanted. I was going to plant beautiful evergreens and flowers that will flourish for years to come. I didn't know much about gardening, but that didn't matter. I knew what I wanted, and I was going to plant to my heart's content.

I looked at the bay window at the front of the house and decided that was a good spot for some evergreens. So, I planted two conical cedars on each side of the window, and in front of them, I added two slow-growing globulars. That left an open spot in the middle, and that is where I put that variegated yellow and green Euonymus mentioned previously.

At the time of the planting, I didn't give much thought to the proximity of the trees to the structure or to the fact that these little trees would not remain little forever. Or that their roots would later be a threat to the foundation of the house.

Sure enough, the trees grew and flourished. In a couple of years, they still looked great, but they were no longer just beautiful. They were now problematic.

For one thing, they were too close to the house. We were now concerned that their root system would damage the house. Second, they were now so big that they blocked the light from coming into the room and prevented the window from opening.

Finally, when it became necessary to replace the windows, we had to cut down both trees to accommodate the new window and allow sunlight into our home. Cutting down those two conical pine trees was a tough decision to make, but it was necessary. Today the two stumps serve as a painful reminder of that decision.

Sometimes, as Christians, we are short-sighted. We make decisions and allow things to come into our lives and crowd out the blessings that God wants to bring into our lives. To allow the blessings to flow, we have to cut down the trees causing the blockage.

This will be painful because you care about the thing causing the blockage, but for God to fulfill His purpose in your life, you will have to cut them down. The pain will go away. And with the obstruction out of the way, you will have a clearer vision. Sometimes in our short-sightedness, we do things without looking at the big picture. Do not allow things to come into your life that blocks what God wants to bring into your life.

> He cuts off every branch in me that bears no fruit, while every branch that does bear fruit he prunes so that it will be even more fruitful.
>
> **JOHN 15:2, NIV**

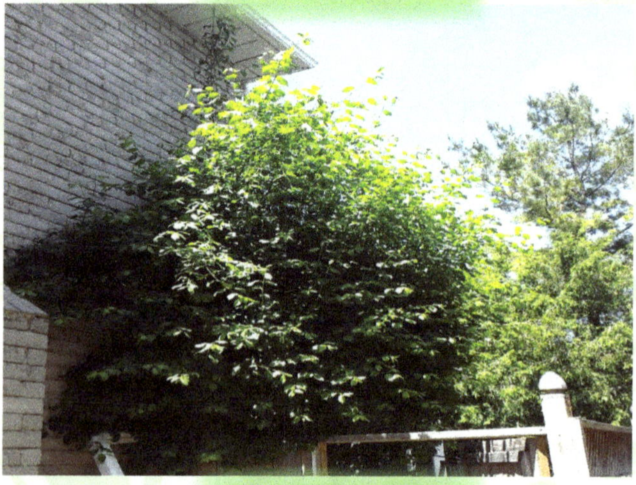

LESSON 9

Insignificant Can Turn Into Something Beautiful

> **But now thus says the Lord, He who created you O Jacob, And He who formed you, O Israel: "Fear not, for I have redeemed you; I have called you by My name; you are Mine."**
>
> ISAIAH 43:1, NKJV

I remember when we moved into our neighborhood, the newness of everything was overwhelming. The evidence of housing construction where once was a wilderness, was very evident. Behind our house was still considered wilderness as it was very bushy and still teeming with wildlife and verdant.

Being new to the area, I went for a walk to explore the bushes in the back of our newly constructed house. I decided to pull up a small seedling and took it home. In hindsight, this was a commemoration since there is no evidence there has ever been vegetation in the area.

There was nothing special about this seedling. It was chosen simply because it was small and allowed me to uproot it with ease. I took it home and planted it at the side of the house without giving much thought to what it would look like as the years rolled on. I cannot remember nurturing it in any way, but over the years, it grew into a beautiful tree that now adds beauty and value to our home.

Over the years, the forest has been replaced with more houses and a school. Had I not rescued this insignificant tree, it would no longer exist. As humans, we are so much like this tree, insignificant and worthless in the grand scheme of things. However, as this tree was rescued, so too were we rescued by the Creator of the universe, who doesn't just plant us thoughtlessly by the wayside, but lovingly plants us in good soil. He continues to nurture us daily with new blessings every morning and then watch over us protectively as we blossom and grow into something beautiful.

" He has delivered us from such a deadly peril, and He will deliver us again. On Him we have set our hope that He will continue to deliver us."
2 CORINTHIANS 1:10, NIV

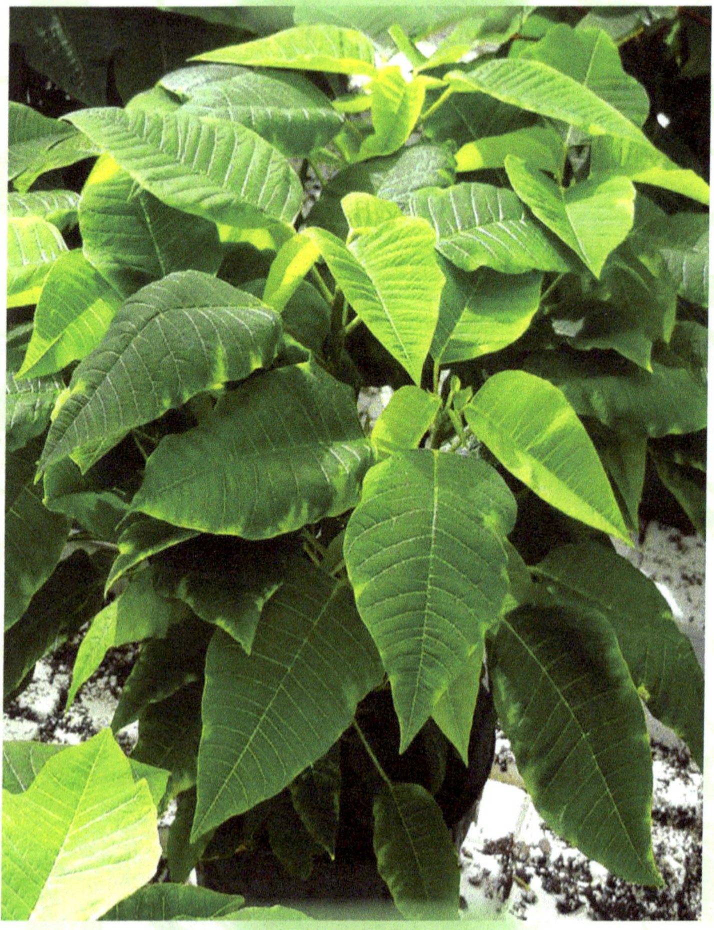

LESSON 10

You Don't Have the Final Word

> **For I will restore health to you, and heal you of your wounds… because they called you an outcast…**
> JEREMIAH 30:17, NKJV

This is the poinsettia I mentioned earlier that I forgot to water. The season was over; the red was gone, most of the leaves had fallen off. I decided it was time to get rid of it.

I have difficulty discarding plants because, somehow, I believe something miraculous will happen, and they will come back to life. So, with that thought in mind, I deposited the seemingly dead poinsettia in the corner of the back patio. Every time I watered the other plants, it also got watered. Watering it became a routine. Before long, I didn't notice the plant, even though it was still in the same spot.

One day in late July, I noticed that the plant was no longer woody. In fact, it looked lush and green. I thought, "Is this the same plant I almost threw away?"

I started thinking about it. I now envisioned the red that is typical of poinsettias coming back in time for me to take it back indoors to be enjoyed for another Christmas season. Isn't that so much like us?

Sometimes we are beaten up by life's circumstances. It appears as if we have had it. Friends and family have written us off, thrown us to the curb, thinking no good can come from us. But God, our heavenly father, never gives up on us.

He looks at us, not at the sorry state we are in at the moment, but at what he knows we can be. He does not reflect on our past accomplishments and compares them to how far we have fallen.

Instead, he sees us for what we can be. He looks beyond our faults and shortcomings and sees our needs. Then in His characteristic goodness, He supplies those needs, so we are able to accomplish the divine plans and purpose He has for our lives.

"The LORD will fight for you;
you need only to be still."
EXODUS 14:14, NIV

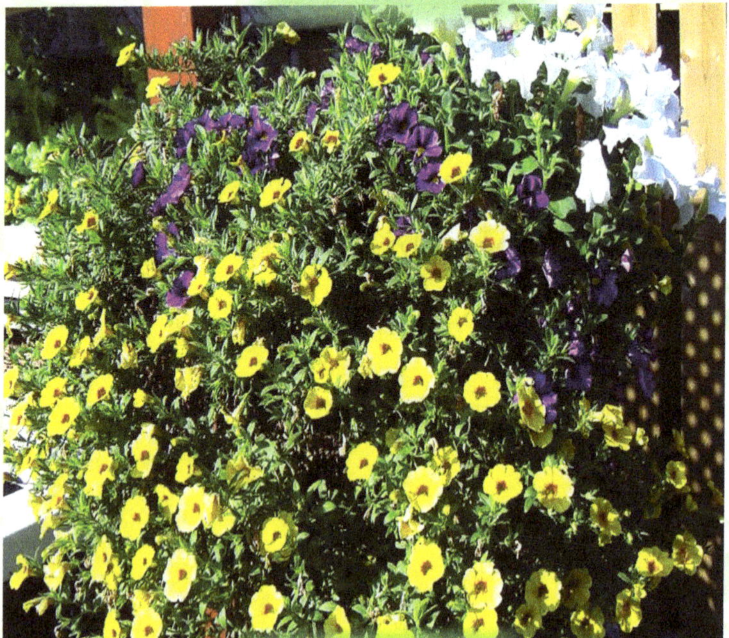

LESSON 11

You Must Be Watered on a Daily Basis

> **Because of the Lord's great love we are not consumed, for his compassions never fail. They are new every morning; great is your faithfulness.**
> **LAMENTATIONS 3:22-23, NIV**

My basket of Petunias looked beautiful, hanging from the end of the patio, resplendent in her purple and yellow hue. I was worried about them at first. They didn't seem as if they would make it, but I kept feeding them, anticipating the day they would reflect the glory they were supposed to. Sure enough, they did, and they looked beautiful.

Every evening, I would water them well, so they had enough water to sustain them during the day when they were in the scorching sun. One evening I came home and was tired, so I went to bed and did not water them. The next day I came home, I did not recognize my plants. They were very badly wilted.

I thought, "Oh no, I killed them!" I ran to the rain

barrel and gave them a thorough drenching. In no time, their vigor was back, and they looked as if nothing had happened.

That's how it is with my Christian life; sometimes, I forget or neglect to feed on the word of God. When that happens, I am spiritually wilted and cannot reflect the glory God intends. I cannot store up the word and expect to be nourished in the coming days.

Like my plants, I need a daily drenching of the Holy Spirit to sustain me throughout the day. As the sun dries up the water from the plants; so too, the devil and the cares of this world will suck the life out of you. Therefore, you must make sure you have a fresh supply of the Holy Spirit's power every day to survive.

> The LORD is my Shepherd, I lack nothing.
> He makes me lie down in green pastures,
> He leads me beside quiet waters,
> He refreshes my soul.

PSALM 23: 1-3, NIV

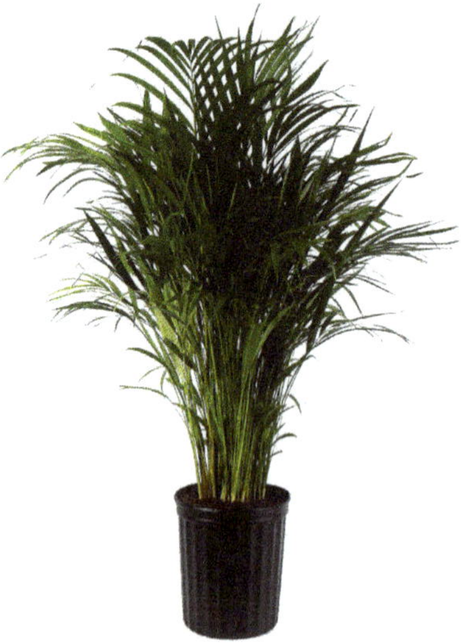

LESSON 12

Are Not Two Sparrows Sold For a Penny?

> **Are not two sparrows sold for a penny? Yet not one of them will fall to the ground outside your Father's care.**
> MATTHEW 10:29, NIV

Refusing to accept that every palm tree I ever bought eventually dies, I had to have this one. It was so beautiful, as they usually are in the store until I bring them home!

I took the palm home. It was beautiful, resplendent, and lush. I placed it in the foyer, under the circular staircase. It was my pride and joy every time I opened the front door. Not only was it beautiful, but it gave the house a tropical feel, which I loved.

I went camping for a week and left it in the care of my husband and daughter. Upon my return, the palm was unrecognizable! They had forgotten to water it, and it had lost its luster. The prongs were now drooping, and the green hue was replaced by a dark, almost dry shade.

I could not believe it had been overlooked, sitting in

the hallway, being passed, literally hundreds of times, on the way to the kitchen, the most frequented spot in the house. After my initial shock and disappointment, I left it outside for a couple of days, thinking, yet again I had succeeded in killing another palm.

While sitting outside, it was drenched many times, both by the garden hose and rainfall. Yet, it sprang back to life. When the weather turned cold, I brought it back into the house and placed it in the south-facing bay window towering above my African violets and flanked by my now blooming Christmas cactus. It looked great.

One night after the Christmas holiday, I came home rather late. Remembering that I had not watered it for a few days, I grabbed the watering can.

The first thing I noticed was that the tips were brown, the telltale sign that it needed water. Then I saw it. There were white fluffs all over the fronds. I had a feeling I knew what it was, but I went to my guidebook to check. Sure enough, my suspicion was confirmed. Mealybugs!

The guidebook gave directions on how to treat this pesky pest. First, use a cotton swab dipped in alcohol and wipe down each frond, then repeat the process in three days. So off I went, wiping each leaf with alcohol until I could no longer see the white fluff.

To add to my mealybug problem, I noticed that little black gnats were coming from the soil. The remedy for that, thanks to my guidebook and prior experience, was soapy water. So, I administered that as well.

While I was doing this time-consuming and laborious exercise, I thought about Adam and Eve's experience. I have always questioned why God did not "Zap" Adam and Eve after their fall and start over. Why not start with a new specimen without having to die, and perhaps this time without the power of choice? I got my answer.

For the same reason, I did not throw the palm away and purchase a new one. The cost of a potted palm is not very much. I could have thrown out the infested palm and gotten a brand new healthy plant. I didn't do that because of ownership. It was my plant, and I was willing to do whatever it takes to give it a second chance.

God chose not to discard Adam and Eve because they belonged to Him. He loved them and wanted to give them a second chance. He loves us, we belong to Him, and that is why He was willing to go to Calvary so that when we become infected with the sin pest, we can be given a second chance.

Thank you, Jesus!

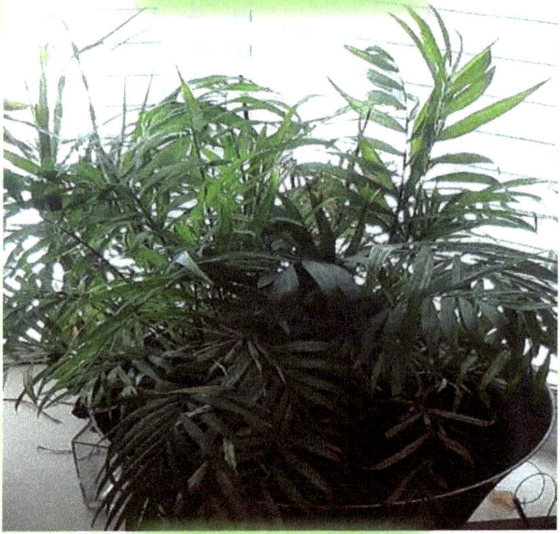

LESSON 13

It's All About Perspective

> *❝...For I have learned in whatever state I am to be content.❞*
> **PHILIPPIANS 4:11, NKJV**

I have long lamented my misfortune and bad luck with palms. Over the years, I have purchased all the different varieties, all with the same result. Eventual death! My solution to the palm tree death is not to buy them anymore. What is the point?

As the saying goes, insanity is doing the same thing while expecting a different result. So, I decided I no longer wanted to be insane, so I will stop buying palm trees. Then it dawned on me.

I would like to think that the Lord spoke to me, and this is what he said. "You don't need to stop buying palm trees. You just need to change your perspective." What do you mean, Lord?

I will tell you; my husband buys me flowers all the time. My favorite flowers are Gladioli. In the summer, you will find multiple vases of different colors all over the house. Sometimes he buys me red roses, and you will find them around the house as well.

Normally when I receive them, I cut the bases off and put them in water, with the package of plant food usually supplied. I figure they will last ten days at the most, and this is with me changing the water every other day. After that time period, they will die, cut flowers eventually do. After they die, I sometimes hang them upside down and keep them around for another little while, or more often, I remove the petals and add them to a large glass vase I keep for petals, prolonging the memories each time I pass the vase.

You see, I expect that my flowers will last only a short time, and while they are alive, I make the most of them and enjoy them as much as I can. So, why not think of palms in the same way? Rather than expecting them to last for years, why not enjoy them the same way I enjoy the cut flowers?

Most cut flowers will last anywhere between 7 – 12 days. Depending on the type of flower and with some tricks and work, you can squeeze in a few more days. Most stores have a warranty period of about three months on palms and other live trees. In other words, if it dies within three months, you can return it to the place of purchase for either a refund or a replacement. If it dies after the warranty period, then you have enjoyed its presence in your home for that period of time. So, I have decided that going forward, rather than complaining and lamenting the death of my palm, I will enjoy it for as long as I can. If it dies, I will take it in stride, the same way I take the death of my gladioli and my roses in stride.

It is amazing how things change when you change

your perspectives. In fact, it is cheaper to buy a palm than it is to buy cut flowers, AND the palms last longer than the cut flowers. However, I was too caught up in grief to recognize that. It is now more than eight months since I purchased my last palm tree, and I am happy to report that it is still alive and looking wonderful.

I will continue to enjoy it for as long as possible, watering and feeding it as I do all my other plants. If and when it dies, I will replace it and start the process over again. What has changed? Just my perspective. That applies to our Christian walk. At times we spend so much time focusing on what we don't have or on the fact that things are not what we would like them to be that we lose sight of the blessings that God gives us daily. You will be able to handle the different seasons in your life and know true contentment in each season with the right perspective.

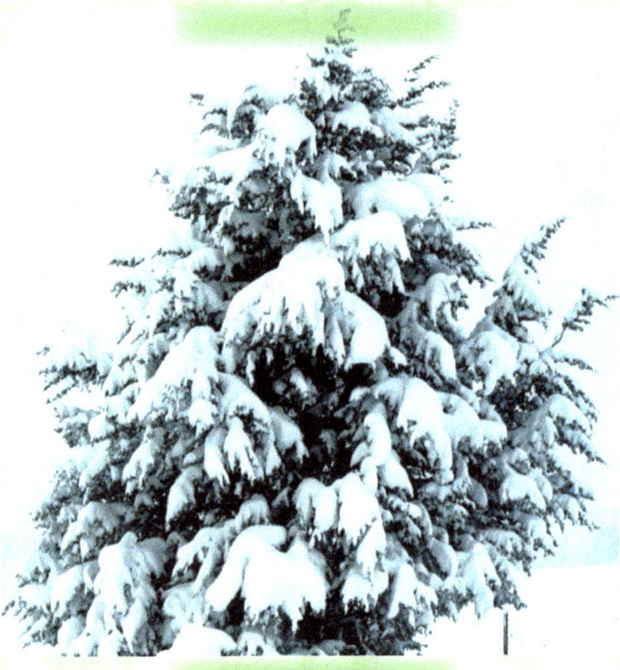

LESSON 14

He Knows How Much You Can Bear

> ❝...God is faithful so He will not let you be tempted beyond what you are able, but with the temptation will provide the way of escape also, that you may be able to endure it.❞
> **1 CORINTHIANS 10:13, NASB**

The winter of 2014 was a brutal one. Not only did we have an ice storm, but we had so much snow that most of the trees on one street in my area were severely damaged due to the weight of the ice and snow. I looked at the evergreen trees on my property and saw the weight of the snow on their branches and felt for sure they would be irreparably damaged. The weight of the snow was so heavy that the branches bent so low they touched the ground. I feared they would break.

I prayed, Lord, please don't let them break. I tried to bring them some relief by literally removing the ice and snow from the branches. However, it didn't take long to recognize that I was doing more damage than good. I was not only removing the snow and ice but was removing the foliage too.

After what seemed like a very long winter, the ice and snow melted, and the branches that were so severely bent went back to their normal position. Unfortunately, many of the deciduous trees on the street had to be replaced because they could not hold up under the extra weight, but I am happy to say the evergreens on my property survived.

In our Christian experience, we will be bombarded with many storms and unpleasant circumstances. Others will be devastated under the same pressures, but we will come through like gold. God promises that He will not give us more than we can bear, but even amid our difficulties, He will make a way of escape for us.

So, when tests and trials come, and they will come. Do not focus on what is happening around you or how others are navigating the tempests. Instead, keep your eyes fixed on Jesus, and allow Him to take you through. When the dust settles, He will make a way of escape for you.

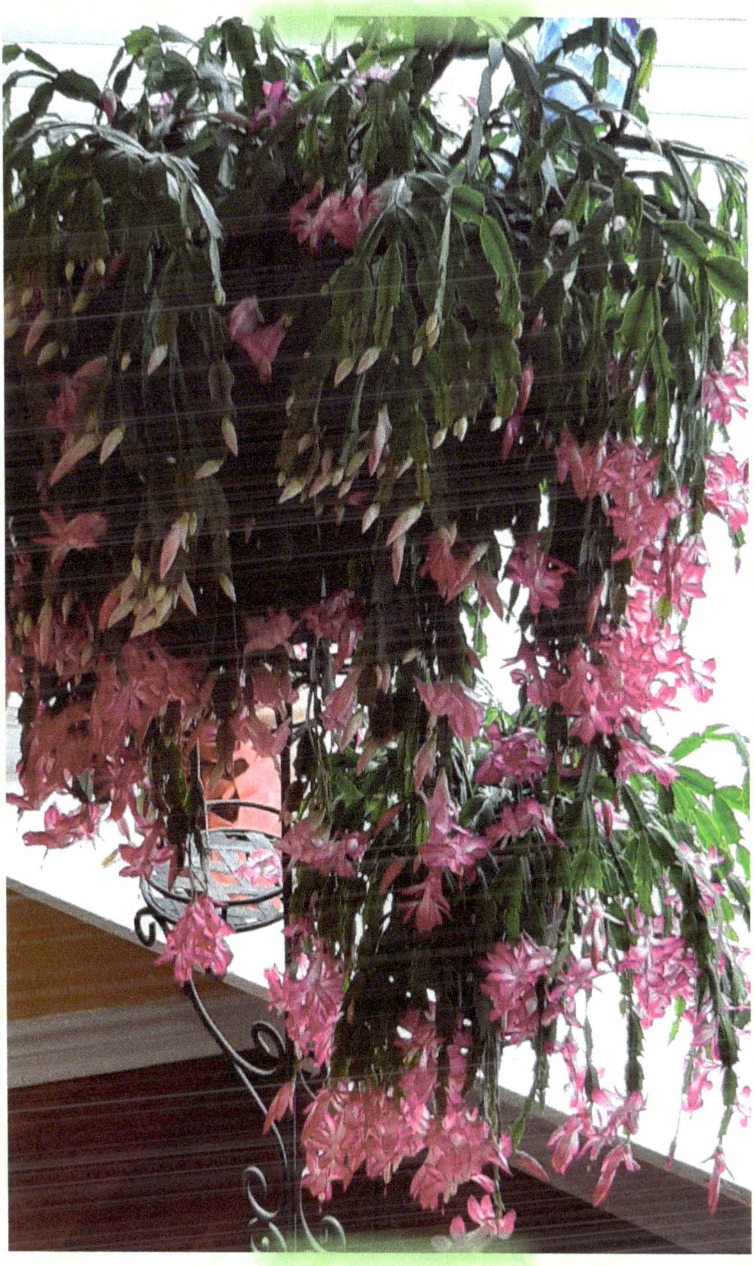

About The Author

Geneitha Allen is a child of God who lives in Ontario with her husband Winston and daughter Candace. She is a visionary, an avid gardener, a self-taught saxophonist, a lover of nature, an active Master Guide, and an aspiring farmer, who for the past few years has been working with her husband in setting the groundwork on their *Journey to a Dream* project.